The Writings of Frithjof Schuon
Series

Songs
for a
Spiritual Traveler

Frithjof Schuon

Songs for a Spiritual Traveler

Selected Poems
German-English Edition

World Wisdom

─────── ❖ ───────

Songs for a Spiritual Traveler
Selected Poems
by Frithjof Schuon
©2002 World Wisdom, Inc.

Library of Congress Cataloging-in-Publication Data

Schuon, Frithjof, 1907-1998
    Songs for a spiritual traveler : selected poems : German-English edition /
Frithjof Schuon.
        p. cm.
    Includes index.
    ISBN 0-941532-31-3 (pbk : alk. paper)
    1. Schuon, Frithjof, 1907-1998 – Translations into English. 2. Religious
poetry, German – Translations into English. I. Title.

PT2638.U915 S66 2002
831'.92—dc21

                                                                    2001057476

Cover: Photograph of Frithjof Schuon in the Swiss Alps

Printed on acid-free paper in Canada

For information address World Wisdom, Inc.
P.O. Box 2682, Bloomington, Indiana 47402-2682

www.worldwisdom.com

Contents

Foreword   *vii*

Songs   2

Index of First Lines   149

Foreword

Frithjof Schuon has long been known as the preeminent representative of the Sophia Perennis, that spring of spiritual wisdom which underlies and penetrates all the world's religions. He was born in 1907 in Basle, Switzerland, of German parents; his father was a violinist of some note, and himself a poet. As a young man, Schuon went to Paris where he studied and worked for a few years before undertaking a number of trips to North Africa, the Near East, and India in order to contact spiritual authorities and witness traditional cultures. In 1959, and again in 1963, he accepted invitations to travel to the American West, where he lived for several months among the Plains Indians, in whom he had always had a deep interest.

During a period of more than 50 years Schuon wrote over 20 books of essays. Originally written in French, they have been translated into many languages, and in themselves comprise a spiritual message of remarkable magnitude. One of the main themes of Schuon's writings was foreshadowed in his early encounter with a marabout who had accompanied other members of his Senegalese village to Basle for the purpose of demonstrating their African culture. When the young Schuon met and talked with him, the venerable old man drew a circle with radii in the sand and explained: "God is in the center; all paths lead to Him."

Schuon began writing poetry in his native German at the age of thirteen. In the 1940's, two small volumes were published privately in Basle, but for many years his published writings consisted almost exclusively of his metaphysical books. It was not until 1995 with the publication of *Road to the Heart*, a collection of poems written in English, that there was any formal presentation of his poetry to the public.

The period of inspiration for the poems in this current volume began in 1995 when Schuon was eighty-eight years old, and continued in a burst of creativity throughout the last three years of his life. When he laid down his pen only a few weeks before his death, he had written over 3,000 poems.

When a collection of his paintings was published in 1992, Schuon stated that "I am not a painter with an interest in metaphysics, but a metaphysician who from time to time produces a painting." His fundamental vocation was always the perennial wisdom as expressed in his written works. This publication of his poetry offers a new and unique opportunity to view his lifelong interest in metaphysical principles and their cosmic and human radiation.

Schuon draws the subject matter for these poems from a deep love of Truth and the sacred. From the time of his earliest childhood he had been drawn to four things: the great, the beautiful, the childlike, and above all, the sacred. Much in his writings and his life can best be understood in terms of this quaternity. As a point of reference we might mention other poets of the past whose works center on man's relationship with God, such as Angelus Silesius, Rumi, Han Shan, and the hymns of Shankara.

The fundamental meaning of Schuon's message is the presence of the sacred in every aspect of our lives and especially in every manifestation of beauty; he teaches, above all, the liberating lesson of "seeing God everywhere and in every thing." Whether he sings of the meeting of man with God, or of life and the range of human emotions and experience — love, grief, knowledge, hope, death — his words point the reader both towards divine wisdom and self-knowledge. His clear and luminous expression of spiritual attitudes and virtues of soul facilitate an unveiling of the intrinsic nature of things.

From this crucial truth he draws for us the necessary conclusion, that of the primacy of prayer in man's life. Through his profound understanding of the soul and compelling descriptions of our relationship with God, he shows us how to live and how to die, how to fulfill our destiny:

> *There is no time in the nature of God;*
> *Nor in the encounter with the Lord.*
> *The moment of prayer is eternity —*
> *It stands in the sky like the morning star;*
> *In the now of the heart lies thy whole life.*

The rich lyricism of Schuon's language communicates not only concepts, but images as well. His poetry reflects his deepest intentions in an explicit and yet musical way, for "in poetry, speech becomes music…" and enters into the soul while feeding the mind in a marriage of unitive harmony. The author calls it "…nourishment for the Spirit and joy for the soul… Precious is poetry that points to the Truth; … And beauty is a symbol that leads us to God." For Schuon, the true purpose of art can only be "an exteriorization that leads to interiorization."

The poetic expressions in this volume offer an insight into the mind and heart of a sage, and one is able to enter more closely into contact with the personality and soul of the author. His poems derive, he says, not from mental effort, but from an interior vision: "I have Paradise written in the ground of my being — I have only to go there to see it." And the creative process, he tells us in several poems, is like stepping into a river — a river of song, whose irresistible current is the love that flows, beyond name and time, from God to God. This is the essence of the art of poetry: to crystallize a formless river of song into finite form, whence what the author has called the "musical crystallinity" of all true poetry. Through the vibrant interplay of formal rigor and musicality, it communicates "a perfume of infinitude through a jewel, by the play of its rigorous facets." This combination, taken together with the spontaneity of inspiration which carries its own necessity, is what enables us to describe the best poets as speaking "the language of the gods."

The inspiration for these poems often woke the author from sleep, preventing him from his rest until words had been put to paper. During the day he kept some small notebooks in his pockets to receive his thoughts as they came to him no matter where he might be. Several times he sought to lay down his pen, thinking he had completed his poetic opus, only to be surprised by a further inspiration.

> One day I wanted to write nothing more;
> The earth, I thought, will go on turning without me.
> Nevertheless, the poems are not the author's work —
> The poet keeps silent; the words write themselves.

When, finally, after three years and almost 3500 poems, he felt his great work completed, he wrote,

> ...whatever we may wish to do:
> Let us follow the call of the Most High —
>
> Let us repose in God's deep Peace.

Originally, Schuon organized the poems as they came to him, into 23 collections of approximately 100-150 pieces each. The books flow with their own natural rhythms and treat a variety of subjects, like a poetic encyclopedia in its richness and vastness. Poems in the earlier collections have titles, while the later ones remain nameless. The selections in this volume have been gathered from nearly all of the collections, and offer a sampling of the themes, styles and breadth of vision found in the complete opus.

Schuon often said that his soul was thoroughly
German. His use of the language evokes both the essence
and the traits of the German character; its elements
permeated his soul and manifested in different modes
depending on the subject at hand. Thus a metaphysical
poem finds its statement in a more classical language; a
poem which speaks to the sentiments sings with the
lyricism and longing that mark the best of German
romanticism; a subject from the wisdom of folklore unfolds
in simple form like a pastoral song from long ago; and a
short, aphoristic poem resounds like a single stroke of a
gong, whose reverberations continue to echo through the
space of our soul, and radiate towards the infinite.

Translations have the effect of tempering, to a
great extent, many of these subtleties and nuances. Schuon
himself was more concerned with maintaining the integrity
of the content than the style of his translations, whether
prose or poetry, and he always preferred a more direct or
literal translation. He considered his poems "didactic" in
nature and termed them "Sinngedichte," or teaching poems.
To this end, every attempt has been made to remain true to
the concerns of the author in providing a faithful rendition
of the meaning, and the intention of this bilingual edition is
to present the original work in all its resonance alongside
the translation.

Why did Schuon write poetry when he had already
expounded his message in his metaphysical books? One can
only reply that a simple reading of these poems will furnish
their own answer, for as with any great artistic production,

theirs is a language at once direct and synthetic, which speaks straight to the heart. Readers familiar with Schuon's many books and articles will find here the same elements that characterize the rest of his vast corpus: universality, essentiality, primordiality; yet in a form that makes his message more easily accessible, and they speak to the heart, the mind, the soul with compelling immediacy. The spiritual traveler may carry this book of "Songs" for a lifetime and not exhaust its content, because its content is the inexhaustibly beautiful life of the spirit.

— The Editors

Da Draußen vor dem Tore,
Da bin ich gern allein,
Horch auf der Vögel Singen
In später Sonne Schein.

Ich hab mich selbst verloren,
Weiß nicht mehr, wer ich bin;
Denn nun das Große Eine
Trag ich in meinem Sinn.

Doch sind so manche Dinge,
Die meiner Liebe wert;
Gott hat mein Herz zum Einen
In seinem Bild gekehrt.

Manuscript page in the author's hand.

Songs

Zum Eingang

Es floss aus meinem Herzen mancher Sang;
Ich sucht ihn nicht, er ward mir eingegeben.
O mög der gottgeschenkten Harfe Klang
Die Seele läutern, uns zum Himmel heben —

Möge das Licht der Wahrheit sich verbinden
Mit Liebe, unsrem Streben zum Geleit;
Und mögen unsre Seelen Gnade finden —

Den Weg von Gott zu Gott — in Ewigkeit.

As an Entry

Out of my heart flowed many songs;
I sought them not, they were inspired in me.
O may the sound of the God-given harp
Purify the soul and raise us to Heaven —

May the light of wisdom unite
With love to accompany our striving,
And may our souls find grace —

The path from God to God — in eternity.

Adastra

Ad astra — zu den Sternen — strebt die Seele,
Die eine ungestillte Sehnsucht drängt.
O Weg der Wahrheit, Schönheit, den ich wähle —
Des Gottgedenkens, das die Seele tränkt.

Du bist das Lied, das alles Sehnen stillt —
Das Gnadenlicht; schein in das Herz hinein!
Der Herr ist unsre Zuflucht, unser Schild —

Sei du mit Ihm, und Er wird mit dir sein.

Adastra

Ad astra — to the stars — the soul is striving,
Called by an unstilled longing.
O path of Truth and Beauty that I choose —
Of God-remembrance that fills the soul!

Thou art the song that stills all longing —
The Light of Grace; shine into my heart!
The Lord is our Refuge and our Shield —

Be thou with Him and He will be with thee.

Bejahung

Was ist es, was die Seel nach Innen ruft?
Was ist das Wunder, dem das Herz begegnet —
Was gibt des Friedens himmlisches Geschenk,
Was ist es, was den Geist von Innen segnet?

Es ist ein Ja zu Gott — ist namenlos,
Hat weder Form noch Grenze, ist sich freun
Am Innersten, am Daseinskern;
                                Es ist
Der Seele Wunsch, in Gott sich selbst zu sein.

Affirmation

What is it that calls the soul inward?
What is the miracle the heart encounters —
What bestows the heavenly gift of Peace?
What is it that blesses the mind from within?

It is a yes to God — it is nameless,
And has neither form nor limit, it is to rejoice
In the most inward, in the kernel of Existence;

                                                  It is

The soul's desire to be itself in God.

Der Schöpfer hat die weite Erdenwelt
In ein Gewand der Rätsel eingekleidet;
Die Schönheit will des Daseins Trug durchbrechen
So wie ein Meteor die Nacht durchschneidet.

Die Wahrheit, die ein Strahl der Gottheit ist
Hat unsrer Seele Dunkelheit gespaltet;
Wohl dem, in dessen Herz des Höchsten Licht
So wie ein Strahl der Morgensonne waltet.

The Creator clothed the wide world
In a garment of enigmas;
Beauty seeks to pierce the illusion of existence,
Just as a meteor cuts through the night.

Truth, a ray of the Godhead,
Has rent the darkness of our soul;
Happy the one in whose heart the light of the Most-High
Reigns like a ray of the morning sun.

Wahrheit und Andacht. Wahrheit ist das Licht
Das gleichsam sich von Gott zur Erde neigt;
Und Andacht ist der Weihrauch, der von uns
Empor zum Allerhöchsten Gute steigt.

Andacht — ein Klang, ein wunderbares Wort,
Duftend nach Liebe und nach heilgem Schweigen;
Ein Zauberwort, des Schönheit schon genügt
Uns von der Wahrheit Macht zu überzeugen.

Der Höchste weiß, was deine Seele braucht
Hienieden, wo du dich der Welt musst beugen —
So sei das Edelharz, das gottwärts raucht.

Truth and Devotion. Truth is the light
That descends from God to Earth;
And Devotion is the incense, that rises
From us to the Highest Good.

Devotion — a sound, a wondrous word,
Fragrant with love and holy silence;
A magic word, whose beauty is enough
To convince us of the power of Truth.

The Most High knows what thy soul needs
Here below, where thou must conform to the world —
So be thou the incense that rises toward God.

Ruf

Weil Du mein Gott bist, ruf ich Dich —
Du wirst mich nicht verlassen.
Du bist der Hort, das Allerhöchste Gut —
Wer kann das Höchste fassen?

Und wenn die Welt in Brüche ging —
Du bist, was mir verbliebe.
Ich weiß nicht, was die Welt ist, was ich bin —
Ich weiß nur, dass ich liebe.

Zeit kann es nicht im Gotteswesen geben;
Auch nicht in der Begegnung mit dem Herrn.
Ewigkeit ist des Betens Augenblick —
Er steht am Himmel wie der Morgenstern;
Im Jetzt des Herzens liegt dein ganzes Leben.

Call

Because Thou art my God, I call Thee —
  Thou wilt not abandon me.
Thou art the Refuge, yea, the Sovereign Good —
  Who can fathom the Highest?

And though the world should fall asunder —
  Thou ever wouldst remain.
I know not what the world is, what I am —
  I only know, I love.

There is no time in the nature of God,
Nor in the encounter with the Lord.
The moment of prayer is eternity —
It stands in the sky like the morning star;
In the now of the heart lies thy whole life.

Das Auge

Ein Auge, das sich öffnet und sich schließt —
So ist das Leben, das euch endlos scheint.
Es strahlt vor Glück, und seine Träne fließt —
Es gibt kein Auge, das noch nie geweint.

Das Auge schauet in die Welt hinein —
Möge des Lebens Blick das Wahre sehen,
Den Gegensatz von Nichts und Licht verstehen —
Möge dein Aug auf Gott gerichtet sein!

The Eye

An eye that opens and then closes —
Such is the life that seems endless to thee.
It shines with happiness, and its tears flow —
No eye exists that never wept.

The eye looks deeply into the world —
So may life's gaze perceive the True, and understand
The opposition between nothingness and Light —
May thine eye direct its gaze toward God!

Morgenrot

Der Morgen schauert über den Zypressen,
Ein letztes Traumbild wird vom Wind verweht.
Die Lerche steigt und singt ein Liebeslied,
Dieweil der frühe Stern am Himmel steht.

Versteh, o Seel, was zarte Schönheit spricht:
Die Güte Gottes ist der Schöpfung Grund.
Dessen sei eingedenk dein tiefstes Herz —
Vom Morgenrot bis zu der letzten Stund.

Dawn

Morning shivers over the cypresses,
A last dream-image is scattered by the wind.
The lark arises and sings its song of love,
While the early star still stands in the sky.

Understand, O soul, what gentle beauty says:
God's Goodness is the substance of creation.
Let thy deepest heart remember this —
From dawn to the final hour.

Da draußen vor dem Tore,
Da bin ich gern allein,
Horch auf der Vögel Singen
In später Sonne Schein.

Ich hab mich selbst verloren,
Weiß nicht mehr, wer ich bin;
Denn nur das Große Eine
Trag ich in meinem Sinn.

Doch sind so manche Dinge,
Die meiner Liebe wert;
Gott hat mein Herz zum Einen
In seinem Bild gekehrt.

Outside, by the gate,
I love to be alone,
And listen to the birds
In the late sun's light.

I have lost myself,
No longer know who I am;
For the Great One alone
I bear now in my mind.

Yet many things exist
That are worthy of my love;
God turned my heart to the One
In the image of Himself.

Vom Selbst

So wie die Funken aus dem Feuer sprühen,
Oder wie Tropfen eines Wasserfalls —
So hat das Selbst sich scheinbar aufgeteilt:
Die Seelen in der Spielerei des Alls.

So ward das Selbst vieltausendmal ein Andrer —
Es ward sich fremd, tief in die Welt verirrt.
Die Wahrheit strahlt — möge die Seel sie finden,
Erleben, bis sie ganz sich selber wird!

Der Geist — er hat sich mit dem Stoff vermischt,
So das Bewusstsein seiner selbst verwischt —
Dies war ein Schicksal, das der Höchste schuf:

Befreit zu werden durch der Wahrheit Ruf.

On the Self

Like sparks that spray out of the fire,
Or like drops of a waterfall,
So has the Self seemingly divided Itself
Into the souls of the Universe's play.

The Self became an "other" many thousand times —
Became a stranger to Itself, lost deep in the world.
But Truth shines — and may the soul find
And experience It, until it becomes wholly itself!

The Spirit mixed Itself with matter,
And consciousness of Itself was blurred —
This was a destiny, created by the Most High:

To be set free by the call of the True.

Urbilder

Geliebte Menschen stehen in den Sternen
Geschrieben, in den tiefen Raum gemalt;
Sie waren schon, bevor sie irdisch waren —
Die Namen Gottes sind ihr Urgehalt.

Sie liebend, liebst du Gott, ob du es weißt
Oder nicht weißt. Gott liebend, liebst du sie —
Denn sie sind Bilder, die der Höchste schuf
Aus seinem Wesensgrund — du weißt nicht wie

Man es soll nennen. Gott ist unermesslich:
Der Eine ist Unendlichkeit — so höre
Das Rätsel — Er ist unergründlich reich,
Ohne dass sich das Eine Sein vermehre.

Archetypes

Belovèd human beings are written in the stars,
Painted in deep space;
They were already, before they were earthly —
The Divine Names are their quintessence.

In loving them, thou lovest God, whether thou knowest it
Or not. In loving God, thou lovest them —
For they are images, created by the Most High
Out of His Nature's Depth — thou knowest not how

To describe this. God is unfathomable:
The One is Infinite — so listen
To the riddle — He is inexhaustibly rich,
Without the One multiplying Itself.

Im Reinen Sein war eine Möglichkeit,
Die sprach: Gib mir das Dasein in der Zeit.
Das Dasein ward erfüllt, da war mein Ich;
Ich sprach: Du bist mein Gott, nun führe mich.
Gott sprach zu mir: du bist mein Ebenbild,
Und du bist frei; zum Wege sei gewillt —
Zum Weg zu Mir; dies ist des Daseins Sinn.
Ich sah, dass ich der Gottheit Spiegel bin.

Ursein, Sein, Dasein, Ich — dem Höchsten zu;
Zum Herzensgrund jenseits von Ich und Du.

In Pure Being there was a possibility,
That said: Give me existence in time.
Existence was granted, and there was my ego;
I said: Thou art my God, now guide me.
God said to me: thou art my image,
And thou art free; say yes to the Way —
The Way to Me; this is the meaning of existence.
I saw that I am the mirror of the Godhead.

Beyond-Being, Being, Existence, I — toward the Most High;
Toward the inmost heart, beyond I and thou.

Die Unterscheidung zwischen Wirklichkeit und Schein;
Die Ansammlung des Geistes auf das Wahre;
Dazu der Seele Edelmut für Gott —
Anderes kann des Geistes Weg nicht sein.

Der Edelmut: Demut und Gottvertrauen —
Du kannst nicht besser auf das Wahre schauen.

Drei Dinge sind mir heilig: erst die Wahrheit,
Und dann, auf ihrer Spur, das Urgebet;
Die Tugend dann — der Seele Adel, der
In Gott auf aller Schönheit Wegen geht.

Discernment between Reality and appearance;
The spirit's concentration on the True;
Together with nobility of soul for God —
The spiritual path cannot be otherwise.

Nobility: humility and trust in God —
You cannot contemplate the True in any better way.

Three things are sacred to me: firstly Truth;
Then, in its wake, primordial prayer;
And then virtue — nobility of soul which,
In God, walks all the paths of beauty.

Sag einmal: Gott — und tausend eitle Taten
Sind ausgelöscht, wie Kerzen, wenn es windet;
Nichts kann dem Unbedingten widerstehen —
Sieh, wie das Eitle vor dem Wort verschwindet.

Beherzige das Wahre in dir selbst —
Sieh, wie des Höchsten Hauch das Herz entzündet.
Wo Gottes Name klingt, da ist der Sieg —
Das Sinnbild, das in Gottes Allmacht mündet.

Say but once: God — and a thousand vain deeds
Are extinguished, like candles in the wind;
Nothing can withstand the Absolute —
Behold how vanity disappears before the Word.

Follow the Truth within thyself —
See how the breath of the Most High kindles the heart.
Where God's Name resounds, there is victory —
The symbol that ends in the Almighty.

So ist es

Mit vielen Dingen leben, selbst ein Ding,
Und doch allein sein in erhabnem Schweigen,
Weil Gott der Eine ist — so ist der Ring
Des Menschseins; Einheit wollte Vielheit zeigen,
Hin und zurück.
              Was soll ich andres reden?
Die Wahrheit ist das ewigjunge Eden
Im Herzen. Kein verfehltes Denken trübe

Das Wechselspiel der Weisheit mit der Liebe.

So It Is

To live with many things, to be oneself a thing,
And nonetheless to be alone in solemn silence,
For God is One — such is the circle
Of the human condition; Unity wished to show diversity,
Flowing forth and coming back again.
                                    What else can I say?
Truth is the Eden ever young
In the heart. Let no false thinking trouble

The reciprocity of Wisdom and Love.

Panakeia

Warum hat Gott die Sprache uns geschenkt?
           Für das Gebet.
Weil Gottes Segen dem, der Ihm vertraut,
           Ins Herze geht.

Ein Beten ist der allererste Schrei
           In diesem Leben.
So ist der letzte Hauch ein Hoffnungswort —
           Von Gott gegeben.

Was ist der Stoff, aus dem der Mensch gemacht,
           Sein tiefstes Ich?
Es ist das Wort, das uns das Heil gewährt:
           Herr, höre mich!

Panacea

Why did God give us the gift of speech?
                    For prayer.
Because God's blessing enters the heart of him
                    Who trusts in God.

The very first cry in this life
                    Is a prayer.
And the last breath is a word of hope —
                    Given by God.

What is the substance of which man is made,
                    His deepest I?
It is the Word that grants us salvation:
                    Lord, hear me!

Nur Ein Mensch steht vor Gott und ruft Ihn an,
Und alle Menschen sind in diesem Einen;
Alle Gebete dieser Erdenwelt
Kannst du in deines Herzens Ruf vereinen.

Alles in Einem — so ist auch die Zeit;
Was ist ein Tag, was ist ein ganzes Leben?
Stehst du vor Gott mit allem deinem Streben,
Dann ist dein armes Jetzt die Ewigkeit.

Willst du nicht für dich selbst zum Gipfel wandern,
Dann sei barmherzig — tu es für die Andern.
Was Erd und Himmelreich zusammenhält,
Ist das Gebet — du schuldest es der Welt.

Only one human being stands before God and invokes Him,
And all humanity is contained within this one;
Thou canst unite all the prayers of this world
In the invocation of thy heart.

All in one — time is like this too;
What is a day, what is one's whole life?
Stand before God with all thy striving,
Then thy poor now becomes eternity.

If thou wilt not journey to the summit for thyself,
Then be compassionate — do so for others.
What holds earth and Heaven together
Is prayer — thou owest this to the world.

Stille

Siehst du die Vögel nach dem Süden ziehn?
So ist Vergänglichkeit: dahin, dahin.
Sei still, verfalle nicht dem Trug der Zeit,
Die einen Traum an einen andern reiht.

Die Sehnsucht strebt nach fernem Anderwärts;
Im goldnen Hier verharrt das weise Herz.
Lass ab vom Traumbild unerreichter Ferne —

Du trägst in dir die Sonne und die Sterne.

Der Weg zum Höchsten Gut ist eine Brücke;
Ich wandere in meiner Erdenhülle
Über den Strom der Welt, doch hör ihn nicht —

Denn meines Herzens Grund trägt Gottes Stille.

Stillness

Do you see the birds migrating to the south?
Such is transience: passed and gone.
Be still, do not fall prey to the deceit of time
Which strings dream upon dream.

Our longing strives for distant elsewheres;
The wise heart abides in the golden Here.
Renounce the dream-picture of unreached lands —

You carry in yourself the sun and the stars.

The path to the Highest Good is a bridge;
I wander clad in my earthly form
Over the river of this world, but I hear it not —

For the ground of my heart carries God's silence.

Die Seel ist ein Geweb von tausend Fragen;
Jedoch die Antwort — sie ist immer da;
Sie wohnt in deiner Brust; sei ihr nicht fern —
Der Allerhöchste ist dir immer nah.

Bejahe Gott, Er wird dein Herz bejahen;
Was du nicht weißt, Er weiß es; du hast teil
Daran in deinem Glauben. Sprich ihn aus —

Im Ja von Gott zu Gott erblüht das Heil.

The soul is woven of a thousand questions;
Yet the answer — it is always there;
It dwells within thy breast; be not far from it —
The Most High is ever near.

Say "yes" to God, He will say "yes" to thy heart;
What thou knowest not, He knows; thou hast a share
In this through thy faith. Pronounce it —

In the "yes" from God to God salvation blooms.

Ich hörte eine Laute in der Nacht —
O süßer Klang des Liedes ohne Worte.
Wer hat so liebevoll an mich gedacht —
Wer stand im Traum an meines Herzens Pforte?

Traumschleier ist die Seele, und gewoben
Aus tiefer Sehnsucht, die nach Liebe drängt;
Schönheit und Liebe sind die Melodei
Die mir des Nachts mein eigen Herz geschenkt.

Des Guten Urnatur will überströmen —
Doch seine Welle, die die Ferne wählte,
Sehnt sich zurück, weg von der Fremde Schemen;

Und so entstand der heimliche Gesang
Der auf den Saiten meiner Seele schwingt

Und letzten Ends aus Gottes Lieb entsprang.

I heard a lute deep in the night —
O sweet sound of a song without words.
Who thought so lovingly of me —
Who, in my dream, stood at my heart's door?

The soul is a veil of dreams, woven
Of longing that yearns for love;
Beauty and love are the melody
My own heart gave me in the night.

The primordial nature of the Good is to overflow —
But its wave, which chose the distant,
Longs to return from the shadows of foreign lands;

And thus was born the secret song
That vibrates through the chords of my soul

And ultimately sprang forth from God's Love.

Ich bin nicht Muslim, Jude oder Christ;
Ich bin der Windstoß, der in Gott erbebte —
Der Geist, der überall und nirgends wohnt;
So sprach ein Sufi, der im Islam lebte.

Jesus: Der Wind — du weißt nicht, wie er weht;
So ist es mit der Seel, die auserkoren —
Mit dem, der aus dem Heilgen Geist geboren.

Der Drang von Gott zu Gott, der nicht vergeht.

I am neither Moslem, Jew, nor Christian;
I am the gust of wind that trembles in God —
The Spirit that dwells everywhere and nowhere;
So said a Sufi, who lived within Islam.

Jesus said: the wind — thou knowest not how it blows;
And so it is with the soul that has been chosen —
With him who is born of the Holy Spirit.

The call from God to God, that never fades away.

Sinnbild

Ein schwarzer Wālī hat mir einst gesagt
Zu Allāh gebe es verschiedne Pfade:
Er sei die Mitte, und die Glaubensform
Sei wie die Speiche an des Geistes Rade.

Und jede Menschenseele ist ein Weg:
Gott wollte tausend Spiegel für das Wahre.
O dass der Mensch in seinem Herzensgrund
Den tiefen Sinn des Einen Seins bewahre —

Des Selbstes, dessen Strahlen zahllos leuchten —
O selig, die das "Ich bin Ich" erreichten!

Symbolism

A black holy man once said to me,
There are different paths that lead to Allāh:
He is the Center, and the different faiths
Are like spokes on the Spirit's wheel.

And each human soul is a Way:
God wanted a thousand mirrors for the True.
O would that man, in his inmost heart,
Protect the deep meaning of the One —

Of the Self, whose countless rays shine forth —
Blessèd are they who reach "I am That I am!"

Heiligtümer

Gebet aus Stein: dies ist das hohe Münster,
Das Innre lang und feierlich und finster —
Ein Fenster, wo das Licht sich bunt zerteilt;
Und Andacht, die vor goldnen Bildern weilt.

Des Islams Bethaus, bilderlos und schlicht —
Nach Mekka strebt der Frömmigkeit Gesicht;
Man steht und betet, Mann an Mann gereiht,
Im Duft des Glaubens, der Ergebenheit.

O Heiligtum jungfräulicher Natur:
Kein Stein, kein Teppich; Wald und Wiese nur,
Und Bergeshöhe, Sonne, tiefe Nacht —
Allüberall die Allerhöchste Macht.

Ein Heiligtum, das Gott uns hat gegeben:
Es ist nicht Fernes, es ist nahes Leben;
Wo sind die Höhen, wo die Götter thronen?
Im Leib des Menschen will die Gottheit wohnen.

Sanctuaries

Prayer in stone: such is the tall cathedral,
Long, solemn and dark within —
A window, breaking the light into sheaves of color;
Devotion, motionless before golden images.

Islam's house of prayer, imageless and plain —
Piety's face is turned toward Mecca;
Side by side, in rows, men stand and pray,
In the perfume of faith and submission to God.

O sanctuary of virgin nature:
No stone, no carpet, only forest and field,
Mountain peaks, sun, and deep night —
And all throughout, the power of the All-Highest.

A sanctuary that God has given us:
It is not far, it is closest life;
Where are the heights where the gods are enthroned?
In man's body the Godhead wants to live.

Natur

O Zeichen der Natur, die uns belehren —
O Schöpferwille, reihend Bild an Bild!
Der Mensch muss kennen, lieben und verehren
Was aus des Allerhöchsten Weisheit quillt —

Und werden, was das tiefe Sinnbild zeigt.
So sieh den Adler: Blitz vom Himmelreich;
Den edlen Schwan auf unbewegtem Teich —
In Demut, die sich vor dem Schöpfer neigt.
Und dann des Löwen königliche Kraft:
Man frägt sich, ob er Kind der Sonne sei.
Und dann der Hirsch mit stattlichem Geweih :
Ein Bild des Heiligen, der Priesterschaft.

Sodann die Göttin in der Form des Weibes:
Sie ist der Gottesliebe Ebenbild.
Die Botschaft ihres wundersamen Leibes
Ist wie der Wein, der uns mit Rausch erfüllt —

Damit dem Weltgetöse wir entrinnen.
O Bilder der Natur, die uns beglücken —
O möge unsre Seel aufs Edle blicken,
Und sei das Äußere ein Weg nach Innen!

Nature

O signs of nature that teach us —
O Creative Will, stringing image upon image!
Man must know, love and reverence
What springs from the Highest Wisdom —

And become what the deep symbol shows.
Consider the eagle: lightning from Heaven;
And the noble swan on the motionless pool —
In humility that bows before the Creator.
And then the royal power of the lion:
One wonders if he is child of the sun.
And then the stag with stately antlers:
An image of the sacred and of priestliness.

Then comes the goddess in the shape of woman:
She is the image of God's love.
The message of her wondrous body
Is like the wine that fills us with rapture —

Whereby we escape the turmoil of the world.
O images of nature that give us joy —
May our souls see what is noble,
And may the outward lead us to the inward!

Wenn der Indianer spricht vom Großen Geist
In Zeichensprache, zeichnet seine Hand
Eine Spirale, die nach oben kreist —
Das Bild ersetzt den rechnenden Verstand.

Die Grundbeziehung zwischen Gott und Welt
Ist keine grade Linie, sie ist Spiel —
Aufsteigend von der Dinge Hin-und-Her
Zum Unbedingten, allen Daseins Ziel.

When the Indian speaks of the Great Spirit
In sign-language, his hand describes
A spiral winding upward —
The image replaces discursive reason.

The relationship between God and the world
Is not a straight line, it is a play —
Rising from the to-and-fro of things
To the Absolute, the goal of all existence.

Der Spiegel

Ist nicht die Welt ein Spiegel, in dem Gott
In tausend Bildern seine Schönheit sieht?
Ein Schauspiel, das vergeht, sich wiederholt —
Aufleuchtet aus dem Nichts, und dann verblüht.

Zweierlei lehren uns des Daseins Früchte:
Die Gottesähnlichkeit, die Gottesferne;
Die Ferne macht des Daseins Stoff zunichte —
Die Ähnlichkeit ist zeitlos wie die Sterne.

The Mirror

Is not the world a mirror in which God
Sees His Beauty in a thousand images?
A spectacle that vanishes, repeats itself —
Lights up from naught, then fades away.

The fruits of existence teach us two things:
God-resemblance and God-remoteness;
Remoteness brings to nothing the fabric of existence —
Resemblance is timeless like the stars.

Nixen

Nixen bezaubern Fischer mit Gesang
Und ziehn sie in die kühle, grüne Tiefe —
So folgt der Weltmensch seiner Leidenschaft,
Als ob ihn eine süße Stimme riefe.

Der Weltliche; nicht so der Geistesmann,
Der alles liebt in Gott, nicht ohne Ihn.
Durchsichtig ist das Gute in der Welt;
Und Gott ist aller Dinge letzter Sinn.

Sag nicht, dass edle Schönheit uns betört —
Nicht den, der ihres Sanges Tiefe hört.

Mermaids

Mermaids bewitch fishermen with songs,
And pull them into the cool, green depths —
Thus the worldly man follows his passions,
As if called by a sweet voice.

The worldly man; not the spiritual man,
Who loves all things in God, and not without Him.
The good in the world is transparent;
And God is the ultimate meaning of all things.

Say not that noble beauty beguiles us —
Not those who hear the depth of its song.

Ātmā

Was du auch lieben magst, du liebst das Selbst
Das in dir wohnt;
In jeder Liebe liebest du das Gut
Das Oben thront;
Und es gehört zu deinem Seelenheil
Dass du es weißt;
Und dass in jeder Lieb dein tiefstes Herz
Den Höchsten preist.

Vom Lieben

Tatsächlich liebt der eine Mensch den andern;
Grundsätzlich liebt er Gott, und weiß es nicht;
Oder er weiß es. Heilig ist die Lieb,
Weil in ihr schläft der Gottesminne Licht.

Ātmā

Whatever thou mayest love, thou lovest the Self
   That dwells within thee;
In every love, thou lovest the Good
   That is enthroned Above.
Part of thy soul's salvation is
   That thou know this,
And that in every love, thy deepest heart
   Praise the Most High.

Loving

When one human being loves another,
In reality he loves God and does not know it;
Or he does know. Holy is love,
For in it sleeps the light of the love of God.

Leila

Säh ich dich tanzen, Leila, wär mein Herz
Verzaubert und gebannt; zum Weg nach Innen.
Säh ich dein Antlitz, hätt ich mich vergessen —
Ich könnt mich nicht mehr auf die Welt besinnen.

Leila: der Engel der Beschaulichkeit —
Ich weiß nicht, ob du Form bist, Melodie,
Ein Liebeslied, ein goldner Märchentraum —
Oder ein Blick aus trunkner Ewigkeit.

Leila

Were I to see thee dance, Leila, my heart
Would be enchanted and spellbound on its inward path.
Were I to see thy face, I would forget myself —
I could remember the world no more.

Leila: angel of contemplation —
I know not if thou art form or melody,
A love song, a golden fairy-tale dream —
Or else a glance from drunk Eternity.

Sein eignes Selbst — als das Unendliche —
Sah Krishna in der schönen Gopis Schar.
Ihr eignes Selbst — doch als das Unbedingte —
Erlebten sie in Krishna, wunderbar.
Und als Er, spielend, ihre Schleier stahl,
Wollt Er Sich sehn in nackter Wahrheit Strahl.

Ātmā und Māyā: Licht und Spiegelschild.
Gott ist die Liebe, und Er liebt sein Bild.

Krishna saw his own self — as the Infinite —
In the throng of lovely *gopis*.
They experienced in Krishna, O wonder,
Their own self — but as the Absolute.
And when, in play, he stole their veils,
He wished to see himself in Truth's naked ray.

Ātmā and *Māyā*: light and mirror.
God is Love and He loves His image.

Werden

Der Traube Saft, gekeltert und gegoren,
Gibt edlen Wein und Rausch. So selbstverloren
Ist eure Seel, wenn sie zur Liebe reift,
Und wenn des Lebens Sinn das Herz ergreift.

Denn was ist Gottesliebe, wenn nicht Wein,
Himmelsgesang — nicht kalter, stummer Stein.
Das Herz ist Eis, das vor der Sonn zerfließt —
Wes Herz zerschmilzt, den hat der Herr gegrüßt.

Verharre niemals in des Zweifels Macht,
Dass der Verstand dir deinen Frieden raube.
Hast du gehört, dass Glaube selig macht?
So sprich getrost: ich glaube, weil ich glaube!

Becoming

The juice of the grape, pressed and fermented,
Yields noble wine and rapture. Thus does the soul
Lose itself, when it ripens unto love,
And when the meaning of life seizes the heart.

For what is love of God if not wine,
Heavenly song — not cold, dumb stone.
The heart is ice that melts before the sun —
Whose heart is melted, the Lord has greeted.

Never remain under the sway of doubt,
Lest the mind rob thee of thy peace.
Hast thou not heard that faith brings salvation?
So say with trust: I believe, because I believe!

Seelengrund

O Nachtigall in süßer Sommernacht —
O Liebeslied, das unsre Seel entzündet!
Wer weiß, wer weiß, was Sehnsucht, Sehnsucht spricht —
Wer hat der Liebe Tiefe je ergründet?

O Liebesleid, das keine Lösung findet;
O Tröstung, die der Erde Schönheit spendet!
O Weltrad, das der Herzen Schicksal wendet;
O Liebestraum, der in das Ewge mündet!

Warum muss in der Süße Trauer sein?
Sie ist in unsre Welt hineingewoben;
Dies ist des Menschenherzens Melodei —

Die Seele sehnt sich, denn sie strebt nach Oben.

Depth of the Soul

O nightingale, in sweetest summer night —
O love song, that inflames the soul!
Who knows, who knows what longing, longing speaks —
Who ever fathomed the depths of love?

O love-pain, that finds no cure;
O solace, that the beauty of the earth bestows!
O world-wheel, that turns the destiny of hearts,
O love-dream, that flows into Eternity!

Why in sweetness must there be sorrow?
It is woven deep into our world;
This is the melody of the human heart —

The soul longs, for it strives toward the heights.

Das Leben

Du wähnst, da sei ein Leben, doch bedenke
Dass in der Tat der Leben viele sind.
Die Zeit verwandelt: warst du nicht ein Kind?
Du wirst ein Greis; dann schließt des Lebens Schenke.

Dann öffnet sich das Tor der andren Welt.
Ist denn ein Erdenleben je gewesen?
Von allem Traumtrug bist du jäh genesen:
Das Wahre leuchtet, und der Wahn zerfällt.

Dein Kern birgt mehr als Lebens kurze Frist;
Gott mag dich leiten — bis du ewig bist.

Life

Thou art deceived in thinking that there is one life;
Think rather that in fact our lives are many.
Time transforms: wast thou not a child?
Soon thou wilt be old, and the tavern of life will close.

Then the door to the next world will open.
Was there ever a life on earth?
Of all dream-deceit thou art suddenly cured:
The True shines forth and illusion shatters.

Thy kernel holds more than life's short term;
May God lead thee — till thou art eternal.

Jugendzeit — schon fern, vorbei —
Wie ein Bilderbuch geschlossen.
Alle Freuden, alles Leid
Sind im Gestrigen zerflossen.

Alterszeit — du nennst es Zeit,
Ist sie doch ein stiller Garten;
Duftend von der Ewigkeit —
Eine Rückschau, ein Erwarten,

Und ein Stehn in Dem, was war,
Ist, und sein wird — immerdar.

Time of youth — already past and gone —
Like a picture book that is closed.
All joys, all sorrows have melted away
Into yesterdays.

Time of old age — thou callest it time,
It is rather a quiet garden,
Perfumed by eternity —
A looking back, an expectation,

And a standing still in That which was,
Is, and shall be — evermore.

Freude

Dies musst du lernen: dich am Höchsten Gut
Restlos zu freuen,
Und von des Lebens ärgerlichem Kram
Nichts zu bereuen.

Du musst es lernen: kindlich dankbar sein
Im Angesichte
Des Höchsten; denn das Gottgedenken macht
Den Kram zunichte.

O Freude, von der Gnade Strahl geschenkt,
Du bist der Morgen,
In dem die Seele neu geboren wird —
Bei Gott geborgen.

Joy

This must thou learn: wholly to rejoice
        In the Sovereign Good,
And to regret nothing
        Of life's vexatious din.

Thou must learn to be thankful like a child
        In the face of the Most High;
For the remembrance of God reduces
        Worldly things to naught.

O joy, bestowed by the ray of Grace,
        Thou art the morning
In which the soul is born anew —
        Sheltered in God.

Stille in Gott — ich könnte endlos dich
In mir besingen. So wie Schönheit Liebe
Erzeugt, so bringst du mir der Liebe Glück —
Auch wenn mir keine Freud erhalten bliebe.

Stille in Gott — du nahst mir stets aufs Neu;
So wird mein Herz nicht müd, von dir zu singen.
So wie die Gnaden, die mir Gott geschenkt,
Von Tag zu Tag in meiner Seel erklingen.

Aus Wahrheit ist das Herz gemacht
In seinem tiefsten Grunde.
Es singt in ihm das Höchste Gut
In gottgeweihter Stunde.

Das Wahre sei der Seele Duft,
Und nicht der Welt Getriebe.
Dein Herze ist die feste Burg;
Drin wohnet Licht und Liebe.

Stillness in God — I could sing thy praise
Inwardly without end. Just as beauty begets love,
So dost thou bring me the bliss of love —
Even if no other joy remained to me.

Stillness in God — thou hast come to me ever anew;
And so my heart never tires to sing of thee.
Just as the graces given me by God
Resound in my soul day after day.

The heart is made of Truth
In its deepest core.
Within it sings the Sovereign Good
In hours consecrated to God.

Let Truth be the soul's fragrance,
Not worldly din.
Thy heart is the mighty fortress;
Therein dwell Light and Love.

Ein Wintermärchen. Schnee bedeckt das Land —
Die Elfenkönigin im Silberschlitten;
Du hörst die Glöcklein, siehst den Wirbeltanz —
Schneeflocken, die von schweren Zweigen glitten.

Schnee — wie ein Leichentuch der Ewigkeit,
Auslöschend alle eitlen Unterschiede —
Als hätte sich auf dies und das gelegt
Das Reine Sein — als ob die Welt verschiede

Oder sich neu gestalte in der Sphäre
Der Ur-Ideen, wo kein Wandel wäre.

A winter fairy tale. Snow covers the land —
The fairy queen comes in her silver sleigh;
You hear the tiny bells and see the whirlwind dance —
Snowflakes, falling from heavy branches.

Snow — like eternity's shroud,
Extinguishing all vain differences —
As if Pure Being had laid Itself
On this and that — as if the world would die,

Or else renew itself in the sphere
Of archetypes, where there is no change.

Ichheit

Beim Rätsel "ich" hat oft mein Sinn geweilt.
Warum bin ich es, der für "ich" sich hält,
Und nicht ein andrer? Warum ist die Welt
In viele tausend Spiegel aufgeteilt?

Doch siehe: niemand ist erstaunt darüber.
Man lebet blindlings in den Tag hinein
Und denkt an manches, nur an dieses nicht;
Man meint getrost: es kann nicht anders sein.

Und dies ist seltsam: dass das Ich sich färbt
Je nach dem Alter, je nach dem Erleben;
Wer bin ich denn? Wer hat mein Herz geerbt,
Wer kann mein Ich aus seinem Kreislauf heben?

Und hinter allem thront das Eine Selbst,
Zutiefst verborgne Sonne unter Schalen
Des Erdenseins.
                        O Sonne, mögest Du
In unsrer Ichheit dunkle Kammer strahlen!

"I-ness"

My mind has often dwelt on the enigma "I."
Why is it I who thinks himself "I,"
And not another? Why is the world
Divided into many thousand mirrors?

Yet see: no one wonders at it.
One blindly lives throughout the day
And thinks on many things, but not on this;
One readily believes it cannot be otherwise.

And this is strange: the I is colored
According to age, according to experience;
Who am I then? Who has inherited my heart,
Who can lift my I out of its orbit?

And behind all is enthroned the Unique Self,
Deep-hidden Sun beneath the shell
Of earthly existence.
                    O Sun, mayest Thou shine
Into the somber cell of our "I-ness!"

Dem Reich der Gnosis gleicht der Sternenhimmel —
Dem Reich der Gotteslieb, der Blumen Lied.
Vom Ewgen zeugt die starre Sternenpracht —
Von süßen Gnaden, was da leuchtend blüht.

Erkenntnisweg — ihm gleicht die stille Nacht,
Weil sie Mysterium ist, Geheimnistiefe;
Der Liebe Weg ist strahlend wie der Tag,
Da er der Seele Liederwelt entfacht.

Gnosis und Liebe — Schweigen und Musik;
Doch beides schenkt das Eine Gottesglück.

The realm of gnosis is like the starry heavens —
The realm of love of God is like the song of flowers.
The rigid splendor of the stars affirms the Eternal —
The shining blossoms tell of sweet Graces.

The Way of Knowledge is like the silent night,
For it is mystery and secret depth;
The Way of Love is radiant like the day,
Because it kindles the song-world of our soul.

Gnosis and Love — silence and music;
Yet both bestow the one divine Beatitude.

Sophia Perennis

Weltliche Philosophen bauen Thesen —
Ein jeder fand, was niemand fand vordem;
Ein jeder hat den Vogel abgeschossen
Mit einem neu erfundenen System.

Der Gnostiker will nur verständlich machen
Der neuen Umwelt, was man früh verstand,
Ja seit der Menschheit Ursprung — eigne Wahrheit
Ist in der Metaphysik unbekannt.

Neu können wohl Gedankengänge sein;
Der Lehre Kern ist zeitlos wie ein Stein.

Sophia Perennis

Worldly philosophers construct their theses —
Each one finds what no one found before;
Each one thinks that he has hit the mark
With a newly invented system.

The gnostic seeks only to explain
In new surroundings what always has been known,
Yea, since the origin of man — individual truth
In metaphysics is unknown.

Forms of thought may well be new;
The doctrine's kernel is as timeless as stone.

Das Schwert

Lass der Wahrheit lichtes Schwert durchschneiden
Nebelschleier deiner dunklen Seele;
Wort des Allerhöchsten und des Heiles —
Trag es stets im Herzen, in der Kehle.

Denke nicht, des Menschen Seel sei heilig
Wenn sie töricht jeden Kampf vermiede;
Den gerechten Kämpfer sollst du ehren,
Denn im edlen Schwerte wohnt der Friede.

Deine Waffe — dies sei wohl verstanden —
Soll nicht eilig eitlen Streit entzünden;
Lass sie mit des Guten Feinde kämpfen,
Falschen Frieden weise überwinden.

The Sword

Let truth's bright sword cut through
The veils of fog in thy dark soul;
The Word of the All-Highest and of salvation —
Carry it always in thy heart and on thy tongue.

Do not think man's soul is holy
When it foolishly avoids every fight;
Thou shouldst give honor to the just warrior,
For peace dwells in the noble sword.

Thy weapon — understand this well —
Should not kindle rash and needless conflict.
Let it battle the enemy of the good,
And wisely overcome false peace.

Glaube

Die Welt, ein tausendfaches Maskenspiel —
    Wer kann es fassen?
Der Weise wird das, was nicht fassbar ist,
    Gott überlassen.

Sieh zu, dass dir kein Rätsel dieser Welt
    Die Ruhe raube —
Gott weiß, aus was die Welt gewoben ist —
    Dein sei der Glaube.

⁘

Securitas — man ist vom Wahn besessen
Es gäbe goldne Sicherheit auf Erden;
Restlosen Schutz gäb es vor Schicksals Launen,
Als könnt das Jammertal zum Himmel werden.

Suche die Sicherheit, wo sie besteht —
Beim Allerhöchsten Gut, das nie vergeht.

Faith

The world, a thousandfold play of masks —
        Who can fathom it?
What is unfathomable,
        The wise man leaves to God.

Take care that no enigma of this world
        Rob thee of thy peace —
God knows what the world is woven of —
        Thine be the faith.

Securitas — people are obsessed with the illusion
That a golden security could exist on earth;
An absolute protection against the moods of destiny,
As if the vale of tears could become Heaven.

Seek for security where it exists —
In the Sovereign Good, that never fades.

Steh du auf deinem Boden
   Den dir der Höchste geschenkt hat —
Lasse dich nicht verwirren,
   Weder durch Außen noch Innen.
Prüfungen muss es wohl geben,
   Sei's in der Welt, in der Seele —
Fest ist der Boden Gottes,
   Und fest sein Wohnen im Herzen.

Wenn wir in dieser Welt nicht leiden würden,
Könnte die Himmelsmacht kein Mitleid haben;
Wäre das Kindlein schon im Paradies,
Wie könnt die Mutter tragen seine Bürden?

Wären wir nicht so hilflos und so klein,
Wie könnten wir in Gottes Händen sein?

Stand upon the ground
        The Lord has given thee —
Let not thyself be troubled
        By the outward or the inward.
Trials indeed must be,
        Both in the world and the soul —
Unshakable is God's ground,
        And steadfast His dwelling in the heart.

If we did not suffer in this world,
The Heavenly Power could not have mercy.
If the little child were already in Paradise,
How could the mother carry its burden?

Were we not so helpless and so small,
How could we be in God's Hands?

Die Krähen fliehen —
Die schrillen Töne brechen durch den Wald;
Herbstblätter schwirren —
O Zeit des weißen Friedens, komme bald.

So ist die Seele —
Wenn Weltgetöse ihre Stille stört;
Wenn keine Gnade
Sich gegen der Gedanken Unrast wehrt.

Der Reinheit Ruhe
Durchdringe unsres Denkens Raum;
In Gottes Nähe —
Die Welt mag Welt sein, doch du hörst sie kaum.

The crows take flight —
Their shrill tones pierce the forest;
        Autumn leaves spiral down —
O, time of white peace, come soon.

        Such is the soul —
When the turmoil of the world disturbs its silence;
        When no Grace
Defends it from restless thought.

        May the quiet of purity
Pervade the space of our thinking;
        In God's nearness —
The world may be the world, but you scarcely hear it.

Beherrschung

Ohn Selbstbeherrschung ist kein Edelmut;
Der Edle muss die Selbstbeherrschung üben
Aus Liebe — nicht für andre, nicht als Zwang;
Sie ist in seinen Seelenstoff geschrieben.

Er liebt sie, weil sie schön und sinnvoll ist;
Weil er nicht Schwäche, noch den Sieg vergisst.

Erhabenheit ist wie die reine Luft
Auf einer himmelsnahen Bergeshöhe;
Gewissheit ist der tiefen Erde Duft —
Das Glück regloser Mitte, wo ich stehe.

Ergebenheit ist meiner Seele Ruh,
Denn was geschrieben steht, lass es geschehen;
Vertraun ist Wandern einem Ziele zu —
Das Glück der Zuversicht beim Vorwärtsgehen.

Mastery

There is no nobility without self-mastery;
The noble man must dominate himself
Out of love — not for others, not as constraint;
It is inscribed in the substance of his soul.

He loves it for its beauty and its meaning;
Because he forgets neither weakness nor victory.

·:·

Serenity is like the pure air
Of a mountain peak close to Heaven;
Certitude is the fragrance of the deep earth —
The happiness of the immutable center, where I stand.

Resignation is the peace of my soul,
For what is written, let it come to pass;
Trust is to move towards a goal —
Going forward in the happiness of hope.

Mir träumt, ein fremder Spielmann stand
Vor meinem Tor
Und sang, und schaute unverwandt
Zu mir empor;
Er sang ein altes Sehnsuchtslied:
Der Liebestrank
War schwerer Wein — als wäre ihm
Das Herze krank.

So ströme immerfort dein Lied
Auf trunknen Saiten —
Ich möcht, mein dankbar Herze könnt
Dein Lied begleiten —
Dir sagen, dass der Morgen nah.
Der Sehnsucht Schöne
Ist wohl Musik; noch tiefer, süßer sind
Des Himmels Töne.

Bald ist am jungen Horizont
Die Sonne da —
Sieh, aller Schönheit Tiefe ist
In Gottes Ja.

I dreamt an unknown bard
Stood at my door
And sang, looking up at me
Unwaveringly.
He sang an ancient song of longing;
Its love-potion
Was heavy wine — as if he were
Sick at heart.

So may thy song stream, unceasing,
Over drunken chords —
Would that my grateful heart
Could accompany thy song,
And tell thee that morning is nigh.
The beauty of longing
Is indeed music; but deeper and sweeter
Are the sounds of Heaven.

Soon on the young horizon
The sun will appear —
Behold, all beauty's profundity is
In God's "yes."

Stella Matutina

Der Morgenstern erhebt sich aus der Nacht
So wie die Göttin Venus aus dem Bade
Des Meeres — eine Perle, dann ein Weib;
Urweiblich ist des Himmels Wundergnade.

Sie ist Geheimnis; sie ist nicht Gesetz,
Sie ist das freie göttliche Vergeben
Tief aus den Wassern der Unendlichkeit —

Und niemand kann der Isis Schleier heben.

Stella Matutina

The Morning Star arises from the night
Like the goddess Venus from the foam
Of the sea — a pearl, and then a woman;
Profoundly feminine is Heaven's wondrous Grace.

She is mystery; she is not law,
She is free divine forgiveness,
From the deep waters of Infinity —

And none can lift the veil of Isis.

Man könnt das Paradies als einen Kreis beschreiben:
In dessen Mitte leuchtet Gottes Gegenwart;
Der Kreis bewegt sich wie ein unermesslich Rad —
So wie der Gopis Ring sich um Shri Krishna schart.

Ein Kreis, der sich vor Gottes Hier verneigt —
Dabei, in trunknem Tanz, nach Oben steigt;
Die Gottesgegenwart: sie ist die Achse, die —
So wie der Stamm die windbewegte Krone trägt —
Bestimmt des Himmelreiches Melodie.

One could describe Paradise as a circle
In whose center radiates God's Presence;
The circle turns, like an immense wheel —
Like the ring of *gopis* gathered round Shrī Krishna.

A circle that bows down before God's Presence —
And also rises in a drunken dance;
The Presence of God is the axis which,
Like a tree-trunk bearing the wind-tossed crown,
Shapes the melody of the kingdom of Heaven.

Urweib und Allweib ist die Heilge Jungfrau;
So ist sie auch das kosmische Erbarmen.
Sie hält den Heimatlosen wie ihr Kind
In ihren göttlich-mütterlichen Armen.

Die Jungfrau: "mit der Sonne nur bekleidet",
So sagt die Schrift. Was mag die Sonne sein?
Das goldne Licht, das aus der Höhe kommt,
Beleuchtend ihre Glieder zart und fein.

Die Jungfrau ist die Wahrheit, unverhüllt,
Schön wie die Liebe und wie Schnee so rein —
Die Sonne ist der Geist, der sie enthüllt
Und so das Wasser wandelt um zu Wein.

The Holy Virgin is primordial and universal woman;
Thus she is also cosmic compassion.
She holds the homeless one like her child
In her divine and motherly arms.

The Virgin: "clothed with the sun alone,"
The Scriptures say. What might the sun be?
The golden light that comes from on high,
Illuminating her limbs, delicate and fine.

The Virgin is the Truth unveiled,
Beautiful as love and pure as snow —
The sun is the Spirit that unveils her
And so transforms water into wine.

Der Sänger

Ihr meint, ich sei der Sänger, weil ich singe —
Weil in der Schönheit ich die Gottheit sah.
Ich bin in einen Strom hineingestiegen —
Der namenlose Sang war immer da.

Das Liebeslied ist jenseits aller Zeit —
Wer kann der Dichtung Zauber voll erfassen?
O ewiger Gesang, o Himmelsstrom,
Geboren aus dem Quell der Seligkeit —

O Andacht, die der Seele Sein vergisst
Und nur noch weiß, was Licht und Liebe ist.

Nebenbei

Dichten ist Botschaft - oder bloße Kunst,
Ein Wörterspiel, vor dem man sich verneigt;
Ich möchte lieber sein ein Bänkelsänger,
Der einen Weg zum Höchsten Gute zeigt.

The Singer

Ye think I am the singer, because I sing —
Because in beauty I have seen Divinity.
I have but stepped into a river —
The nameless song was ever there.

The love song is beyond all time —
Who can fathom the magic of poetry?
O eternal song, O heavenly stream,
Born of the fountainhead of bliss —

O devotion, that forgets the soul's existence,
And now knows only Light and Love.

By the Way

Poetry is a message — or else merely art,
A play of words, before which one bows;
I would rather be a minstrel in the streets
Who proclaims a way to the Highest Good.

Yabyum

In Tibets Kunst: das goldne Götterpaar —
Die Beiden in der Liebe fest umschlungen;
Der Liebesgott, die Weisheitsgöttin: und
Ein jeder von dem Andern tief durchdrungen.

So soll es sein: die Wahrheit und der Weg
Sind eins — das Eine muss im Andern leben.
Die Wahrheit kann nicht bloß im Denken sein;
Der Wille kann nicht ohne Wahrheit streben.

Yab-Yum

In Tibet's art: the golden Divine Pair —
The two locked close in love's embrace;
The god of love and wisdom's goddess:
Each deeply permeates the other.

Thus it should be: Truth and Way
Are one — the one must live in the other.
Truth cannot dwell in thought alone;
And Will cannot strive without Truth.

Die Gabe

Des Wahren Strahlung, heißt es, ist im Schönen,
Es will der Weisheit Tiefe offenbaren;
Und andrerseits strebt Schönheit hin zum Wahren —
Es liegt in ihr, sich nach dem Licht zu sehnen.

Die schöne Königin von Scheba reist
Zum weisen König der Hebräer hin:
Du, Weiser, gib mir, was von Gott du weißt —
Ich will dir alles geben, was ich bin.

Die Wahrheit schenkt uns Gottes Nektar ein —
Wir schulden ihr das Ganze — unser Sein.

The Gift

The splendor of the true, it is said, is in the beautiful,
Which wants to manifest the depth of wisdom;
Yet beauty also strives towards truth —
It lies in its nature to yearn for the light.

The fair Queen of Sheba journeyed
To the wise King of the Hebrews:
"Thou, wise man, give me what thou knowest of God —
I shall give thee all that I am."

Truth pours out God's nectar for us —
We owe it everything — our very being.

Stellvertretung

Sieh einerseits: du stehst allein vor Gott;
Einsam, doch unter seiner Gnade Stern.
Sieh andrerseits: ein gotterfüllter Mensch
Steht groß vor dir, durchleuchtet von dem Herrn.

Ein Himmels-oder Erdenmensch: ein Ort
Der Gottesgegenwart, ein hohes Wort.
Du willst dich reinen Sinns zur Gottheit kehren —
Du musst auch seine edlen Spuren ehren.

Wenn euch die Meister Gottes Wahrheit geben,
Sollt ihr in ihnen Gottes Sein erleben.
Sinnbild ist Urbild. So vergesset nicht:
Der Schein des Mondes ist der Sonne Licht.
Du magst dich neigen vor dem Heilgenschein —

Du neigest dich vor Gott — vor Gott allein.

Representative

On the one hand, you stand alone before God;
Alone, but beneath the star of His Blessing.
On the other hand: a God-filled human being
Stands great before you, illumined by the Lord.

A heavenly or earthly being: a place
Of divine Presence, a lofty Word.
You wish to turn with pure mind toward God,
Then you must honor His noble traces too.

When the Masters give God's Truth to you,
You should feel and see in them God's Being.
The symbol is the image of the Essence. So forget not:
The moon shines with the light of the sun.
You may bow down before the light of holiness —

You bow down before God — before God alone.

Urmensch

Des Daseins Grund: es gibt ein Urbild Mensch,
Das unbewegt in Gottes Geiste schwebt —
Ganz unberührt von allem, was der Leib,
Mit ihm die Seel, im Erdentraum erlebt.

Dies ist der Mensch: platonische Idee,
In Gottes Geist und Güte eingeschlossen —
Und dann in tausend Wesen umgegossen;
Das Leben: Frühlingsblüten, dann der Schnee —

Ein Alles und ein Nichts. All insofern,
Als wir in Gottes Weisheit sind ein Stern;
Ein Nichts, sofern wir stehen in der Welt
Vor Gott, des Macht der Dinge Sein enthält.

Urmensch: nicht bloß ausschließend ist der Sinn:
Der Einzige ist alles, was ich bin.
Sieh, wie der Dinge Rätsel sich verzweigen —

Das Wort muss sein.
Wahrheit durchbricht das Schweigen.

Archetypal Man

The ground of existence: there is a human archetype
That floats, unmoved, within God's Spirit —
Wholly untouched by everything our bodies
And souls experience in the earthly dream.

This is man: a Platonic idea
Enclosed within the Spirit and Goodness of God —
And then recast into a thousand beings;
Our life: first spring flowers, then snow —

An all and a nothing. An all, inasmuch
As we are stars in God's Wisdom;
A nothing, inasmuch as we stand in the world
Before God, whose Might contains the being of things.

Archetypal man: the meaning is not merely exclusive:
The One and Only is all that I am.
See how the enigma of things unfolds —

The Word must be.
                    Truth pierces through Silence.

Das Weltrad dreht sich, und du bist die Mitte
Weil du den Geist trägst, der das All enthält
Und göttlich ist, ohn Anfang, ohne Ende;
Da wo der Punkt ist, ist die ganze Welt.

Caritas

Du, der du einsam betest, denke nicht
Du seist allein; auch andern gegenüber,
Die du nicht kennst, ist dein Gebet ein Gut
Und eine Segenskraft und eine Pflicht.

Gottesgedenken schuldest du dem Höchsten —
Und dann dir selbst, und ebenso dem Nächsten.

Der Ort, wo für den Herrn ihr stillesteht,
Ist wie ein Pol, um den die Welt sich dreht.

The world-wheel turns, and thou art the center
Because thou carriest the Spirit which contains the universe
And which is divine, without beginning, without end;
Where the point is, there is the whole world.

Caritas

Thou who prayest in solitude, think not
Thou art alone; for others too,
Whom thou knowest not, thy prayer is a good
And a benediction and a duty.

God-remembrance thou owest to the Most High —
Then to thyself, and likewise to thy neighbor.

The place where ye stand still before the Lord
Is like a pole round which the world is turning.

Die Flucht

Die Menschen scheinen auf der Flucht zu sein —
Was ängstigt sie, was macht wohl, dass sie fliehn?
Sie fliehn nicht nur vor Fremdem, das bedroht,
Sie fliehen vor sich selbst, vor ihren Mühn —
Vor ihrem bloßen Dasein. Mensch, hör zu —
Du bist am Rand des Seins, wo gehst du hin?
Halt ein!
            Gott ist die Mitte und die Ruh.

Habt ihr gesehen, wie die Seifenblase
In zarten Farben schillernd, steigt und fällt,
Nach oben schwebt, dann sich verliert im Grase
Und nicht mehr ist — so ist es mit der Welt

Und mit dem Leben. Nicht mit unserm Herzen
Das Gott gesehn. So wie im heilgen Schrein
Andächtig reglos die geweihten Kerzen
Vor Gott stehn — so wird auch dein Herze sein.

---- ⋱ ----

Flight

Men always seem to be fleeing —
What frightens them, what makes them flee?
They flee not only from strange things that threaten,
They flee from themselves, from their woes —
From their very existence. Listen, O man,
Thou art at the rim of Being, where dost thou go?
Halt!
       God is the Center and our Repose.

---- ⋱ ----

Have you seen how the soap bubble
In delicate, shimmering colors rises and falls,
Floats upward, then is lost in the grass
And is no more — so it is with the world

And with life. But not with the heart
That has seen God. Just as in a holy shrine
The consecrated candles stand motionless in devotion
Before God — so shall thy heart be also.

In einer Welt, wo aller Glaube schwindet,
Wird Gott den Menschen, die noch gläubig sind,
Ganz ohne Maß verzeihen; so verzeiht
Die vielbesorgte Mutter ihrem Kind.

In schweren Zeiten ist ein gutes Zeichen –
Leicht wird es sein, den Himmel zu erreichen.

Mysterium der Geduld: Leid und Verdruss
Die unsre müde Seele tragen muss
Im Strom der Stunden und im Strom der Tage –
Und jeder Tag hat seine eigne Plage.

Geduld: genährt von einer innern Quelle
Die keine Zeit kennt; Tröstung, stets zur Stelle,
Von Innen her geschenkt – von Oben her;
Die Last ist leicht – Gott trage, was zu schwer.

In a world where all faith is disappearing,
God will forgive without measure
Those who are still believers,
Just as an anxious mother forgives her child.

In hard times, there is a good sign:
It will be easy to reach Heaven.

Mystery of patience: the sorrow and vexation
That our weary soul must bear
Through the river of hours, through the river of days —
And each day has its own affliction.

Patience: nourished by an inner source
That knows no time; solace ever present,
Bestowed from Within — from Above;
Light is the burden — let God carry what is too heavy.

Stelle dir nicht die Frag: was wird geschehen?
Lasse die Dinge kommen, wann sie kommen
An dich heran; sei ruhig in dem Jetzt
Das Gott gehört; der Glaube wird dir frommen.

Wenn die Gedanken sich zum Höchsten wenden,
Ist Er bei dir; und das, was vor dir liegt
In Welt und Jenseits, ist in seinen Händen.

Der Friede Gottes wartet vor der Tür
Des Herzens, dass du sie wohl öffnen mögest
Mit deinem Glauben, der Gewissheit trägt —
Der nicht nach dem Warum der Gnade frägt.

Do not ask thyself what is going to happen.
Let things come to thee the way
They will; be at peace in the Now
That belongs to God; thy faith will reward thee.

If thy thoughts turn to the Most High,
He is with thee; and what lies before thee,
In this world and the next, is in His Hands.

The Peace of God is waiting at the door
Of thy heart, waiting for thee to open it
With thy faith, which carries certitude —
And does not ask about the why of Grace.

Sie denken an Gott und sie zählen
Gebete bei flackerndem Licht;
Sie drehen die heiligen Perlen
Mit Fleiß, bis der Faden zerbricht.

Hoch oben singt eine Lerche
Voll Freude vor Gottes Gesicht;
Sie trillert, sie steiget zum Himmel —
Sie zählt ihr Gejubel nicht.

Sagt doch Sankt Bernhard: die Liebe
Ist, weil sie Liebe ist.
Und selig, wer beim Lieben
Das Zählen — sich selbst vergisst.

They think of God and count
Their prayers in the flickering light;
They turn the holy beads with diligence,
Until the thread breaks.

High above a lark is singing,
Full of joy before God's Face;
It trills as it rises in the sky —
It does not count its jubilations.

For St. Bernard has said:
Love is, because it is love.
And blessèd he who in loving
Forgets counting — and forgets himself.

Der Schleier

Traumschleier Welt: wer kann dein Spiel verstehen?
Ein Wunderwerk aus tausend Traumgeweben,
Oft wild bewegt wenn Schicksals Winde wehen;
Wer kann der dunklen Isis Schleier heben?

Denn dies Gewand verbirgt und offenbart;
Du siehst nicht das Geheimnis, doch der Wille
Des Schöpfers zeigt sich in der bunten Fülle,
Die sich um unsichtbare Mitte schart.

Was ist in alledem der letzte Sinn?
Die Äußerung zur Innerung: wir sollen
Bewirken, wenn des Daseins Bilder rollen,
Dass sie uns — gebe Gott — nach Innen ziehn.

Woher wir kommen und wohin wir gehen
In dieser Träumerei? Du sollst nicht fragen.
Das Weltrad mag sich um das Eine drehen —
Dieweil wir letztes Sein im Herzen tragen.

The Veil

Dream-veil world: who can understand thy play?
A wondrous work woven of a thousand dreams,
So often wildly stirred when the winds of destiny blow;
Who can lift the veil of the dark Isis?

For this garment at once covers and reveals;
Thou canst not see the secret; but the Creator's
Will shows Itself in the colorful fullness
That gathers round the unseen Center.

What is the ultimate meaning in this?
Outwardness in view of inwardness:
As the images of existense roll past,
We must cause them — God willing — to draw us inward.

Whence do we come and whither do we go
In all this dreaming? Thou shouldst not ask.
The world-wheel may circle round the One —
All the while we carry ultimate Being in our heart.

Raum-Zeit

Unendlich ist der Raum, die Zeit —
    Wir können's nicht erfassen.
Wir müssen uns in ihrem Bann
    Durchs Leben tragen lassen.
Wir wissen nicht, was beide sind —
    Nur, dass sie Gott beweisen.
Denn da sie da sind, ist gewiss,
    Dass sie den Herrn umkreisen.
O Wunder, dass es in der Welt
    Bewusstsein gibt und Minne —
Dass in des Alls Unendlichkeit
    Ein Herz das Heil gewinne.

Space-Time

Space and time are infinite —
            We cannot fathom them.
Throughout life, we must let ourselves
            Be drawn into their spell.
We do not know what either is —
            Only that they prove God.
And certain it is, since they exist,
            They circle round the Lord.
O wonder, that in the world there is
            Both consciousness and love —
That in the All's infinity
            A heart may win salvation.

Vergleiche

Ein Sonnenstern — unvorstellbare Größe;
Ich bin ein Sandkorn, das im Raum verschwindet.
Und dennoch trage ich den Stern in mir —
Er ist ein Stäubchen, das mein Geist begründet.

Denn alles Dasein ist aus Geist geboren;
Und dieses Wunder hat mir Gott geschenkt.
Gott wollte in der Welt als Zeuge leben
Und hat sein Alles in mein Nichts versenkt.

Des Menschen Sein ist mehr, als was du weißt —
Denn keinen Maßstab gibt es für den Geist.

Schönheit ist Geist — zu edler Form geronnen;
Geist hat den Stoff besiegt — für sich gewonnen.

Gewaltig scheint die Welt, die uns umgibt —

Noch größer ist, wer seinen Schöpfer liebt.

Comparisons

A sun star — unimaginably great;
I am a grain of sand that vanishes in space.
Yet I carry the star within me —
A speck of dust, and my spirit is its foundation.

For all existence is born of the Spirit,
And God has bestowed this miracle on me.
God wished to live in the world as a witness,
And so He cast His All deep into my naught.

Man's being is more than what thou knowest —
There is no measuring rod for the Spirit.

Beauty is Spirit, crystallized into noble form;
Spirit has vanquished matter, and won it for Itself.

Immense seems the world surrounding us —

Greater still is he who loves his Creator.

Yin-Yang

Ein schwarzer Punkt in einem weißen Feld,
Und umgekehrt: ein weißer Punkt im Dunkeln.
In diesem Wechsel liegt die ganze Welt;
Sieh wie der Formen viele Seiten funkeln.

Erkenne wohl das Wechselspiel der Dinge:
In jedem findest du etwas vom andern.
Du magst das grenzenlose All durchwandern:
Die Wahrheit liegt auf einer scharfen Klinge.

Darüber strahlt das Tao, höchstes Licht —
Ganz ohne Gegensatz, das Große Eine.
Du willst es fassen, es gelingt dir nicht —

O dass die Weisheit Tag und Nacht vereine:
Wort und Geheimnis. Bleibe, was du bist —
Im Einen wirst du schauen: Das, was ist.

Yin-Yang

A black dot in a white field, and
The converse: a white dot in the dark.
The whole world lies in this exchange;
See how the many facets of forms are shining.

And recognize the interplay of things:
In each you find something of the other.
Well may you wander through the boundless All —
The Truth lies on a blade's edge.

Above it shines the Tao, sublime light —
Wholly without opposite, the Great One.
You wish to grasp it, but do not succeed —

O that wisdom may unite day and night:
Word and mystery. Remain what you are —
In the One you will see That which is.

Lallā

Als Lallā Yogīshwarī Ātmā fand
In ihrem Innern, war die Aussenwelt
Für sie ihr einzig Kleid, ein Traumgewebe;
So ging sie nackend unterm Himmelszelt.

So wie von außen sie nach Innen drang,
So drang das Innre in des Leibes Fülle;
So ging sie nackt und tanzend durch das Land
Im Rausche Lakshmīs und in Ātmās Stille.

Lallā

When Lallā Yogīshwarī found *Ātmā*
Within herself, the outer world became
Her sole garment, a web of dreams;
Thus she went naked beneath the vault of Heaven.

And as she entered from the outward to the Inward,
So did the Inward enter her body's fullness;
And thus she went naked and dancing through the land —
In Lakshmī's ecstasy and in *Ātmā's* stillness.

Shánkara

Sie, die des Denkens Fluss zum Schweigen bringt,
Göttlich besänftigend der Seele Sinn —
Sie ist Benares, ist die heilge Stadt;
Sie ist es, die ich liebe — die ich bin.

Ich bin die große Stille nach dem Tosen,
Nach Weltmeers wildbewegter Melodie —
Sprich: Friede, Friede; Herz, du bist das Selbst

Om, Shānti, Shānti; aham Brahmāsmi.

Des ganzen Veda ungeheurer Strom
Ist in der Einen heilgen Silbe Om.
Sprich Om, sagt Shánkara — was willst du mehr?
Im kleinsten Wassertropfen ist das Meer.

Shankara

She, who brings the stream of thought to silence,
Divinely giving peace to our soul —
She is Benares, the sacred city;
It is She that I love — and that I am.

I am the great Stillness after the storm,
After the world-sea's wild melody —
Say: Peace, Peace; heart, thou art the Self —

Om, Shānti, Shānti; aham Brahmāsmi.

The immense river of the whole Veda
Lies in the one sacred syllable Om.
Say Om, said Shankara — what more dost thou wish?
In the smallest drop of water is the sea.

Dein Name ist ein wundersamer Laut
        Und dennoch Stille;
So lass mein Herz sich öffnen, dass es sich
        Mit Licht erfülle.
Mein Wort, Herr, ist Gebet — ein tiefer Klang
        Und dennoch Schweigen;
Und möge sich mein Herz durch Deine Gnad
        Nach Innen neigen.

Du bist mein Gott, und ich rufe Dich —
Ich rufe Dich, der Du der Herr bist.
Mein Geist ist Dir nah im Ewigen Jetzt —
Im Lichte, das jenseits der Zeit ist.
Ich sag: "Ich bin klein, mein Herz ist rein" —
Ich wollte als Kind schon bei Dir sein.

Thy Name is a wondrous sound
        And yet stillness;
So let my heart open itself, that it may
        Be filled with light.
My word, O Lord, is prayer — a deep sound
        And yet silence;
And may my heart through Thy Grace
        Turn toward the inward.

Thou art my God, and I call Thee —
I invoke Thee, who art the Lord.
My spirit is near Thee in the Eternal Now —
In the Light, which is beyond time.
I say: "I am small, my heart is pure" —
Already as a child I wished to be with Thee.

Besinnung

Gespräch mit Gott. Er wird dir Antwort geben,
Oder sein Schweigen wird dir Antwort sein;
Denn Er ist bei dir; du bist nie allein.
In seiner Stille mag dein Herz erbeben —

Und lauschen, was der Name Gottes spricht.
Du ahnest, wie des Himmels Gärten blühen;
Du hörst des Urseins tiefe Melodien —

Den Urgesang von Liebe und von Licht.

Meditation

Talk to God. He will answer thee,
Or else His Silence will be an answer;
For He is with thee; thou art never alone.
In His Stillness may thy heart be stirred —

And listen to what the Name of God is saying:
Thou canst divine how Heaven's gardens bloom;
Thou hearest the deep melodies of primordial Being —

The primal song of Love and Light.

Gegrüßt sei mir der tiefe, wilde Wald —
Gewundner Weg bergab zu einem Bach;
Tief eingeschnitten ist das dunkle Tal —

Du hörst wie eines Vogels Lied verhallt
Und sitzest hin auf eines Baumes Stumpf,
Allein und in Besinnung. Stille Stunden —

Du steigst zurück, zögernd und durch Gestrüpp,
Auf einem Pfad, der sich zum Licht gewunden.

Wald: Heiligtum der Wildnis — die Natur
Raunt ihr Geheimnis auf der Gottheit Spur.

Let me greet the deep and wild forest —
A winding path down to a brook;
Deeply carved is the dark valley —

You hear how a birdsong fades away,
And sit on a tree stump,
Alone and in contemplation. Quiet hours —

You climb back up, hesitating through the brush,
On a trail that winds up to the light.

Forest: sanctuary of wilderness — nature
Whispers its secret in the tracks of Divinity.

Ich lebe jetzt, in diesem Augenblick —
In keinem andern;
Mit allen Wesen, Dingen, die mit mir
Durchs Weltall wandern.

Was für mich jetzt ist, ist auch jetzt für andre,
Große und Kleine;
Ausnahmen im gewaltgen Strom der Zeit —
Man kennet keine.

Ein jeder Augenblick, der mir entflieht,
Ist Weltgeschichte;
Ein jeder macht das Jetzt, das vor ihm war,
Rastlos zunichte.

O gebe Gott, dass ich im Ewgen Jetzt
Die Ruhe finde;
Dass ich den Sinn all dessen, was wir sind,
Im Herz ergründe.

I live now, in this instant —
And in no other;
With all the creatures and things which journey
Through the universe with me.

What for me is now, is now for others too,
Great and small;
There are no exceptions, none at all,
In the powerful stream of time.

Each moment that flies from me
Is history;
Each moment ceaselessly destroys the now
That went before it.

God grant that I find peace
In the eternal Now;
And discover in my heart
The meaning of all we are.

Das Leben, sagt man, geht dem Tod entgegen;
Nicht so — das Leben strebt zu Gott allein.
Man sagt ja nicht, man gehe nur zur Tür,
Wenn man zu Gast beim König könnte sein.

Was vor dem Tode kommt, ist Gottes Wille;
Was nachher kommt, ist seiner Gnade Fülle.

Geburt und Tod — zwei Ufer und ein Meer
Dazwischen, das wir überqueren müssen;
Wo kommst du her, o Mensch, wo gehst du hin?
Wer wird dich nach der langen Fahrt begrüßen?

Geburt und Gott — der Weg vom Nichts zum Sein;
Nichts, Dasein, Sein — du bist auf Daseins Wogen,
Es scheint dir alles schwankend. Doch der Kahn
Wird von der Gnade Hand zu Gott gezogen.

Life, it is said, is a movement towards death;
Not so — life flows towards God alone.
One hardly says that one goes only to the door,
When one could be a guest of the King.

What comes before death, is God's Will;
What comes after, is the fullness of His Grace.

Birth and death — two shores, and a sea
Between them we must cross;
Whence comest thou, O man, and whither dost thou go?
Who will greet thee at thy long journey's end?

Birth and God — the path from nothingness to Being;
Nothingness, Existence, Being — thou art tossed upon
The waves of existence, everything seems to sway.
But the boat is drawn towards God by the hand of Grace.

Wiederkehr

Dasein, dann nicht mehr dasein; Wirklichkeit,
Und nachher nichts; ein Trost, der von uns schied,
So wie ein ungehörtes Liebeslied
Im Zeichen eilender Vergänglichkeit
Bei Nacht verklingt.
          Jedoch ein Weiser sprach:
Du trauerst, weil die Welt verwelkt; sei wach
Und klage nicht; denn Gott enttäuscht uns nie.
Bei Ihm ist alles, was der Liebe wert,
Und was in neuer Strahlung wiederkehrt —
Ja aller Schönheit tiefste Melodie.

Und wisse: alles Gute, das vergeht,
Ist so beschaffen, dass es aufersteht.

Return

To exist, then to exist no more; reality,
Then nothing; a solace that has left us,
Just as a love song never heard
Marked by the sign of fleeting transcience
Dies away in the night.
                    And yet a wise man said:
You mourn because the world is fading; be wakeful
And lament not, for God never fails.
With Him is all that is worthy of love,
And that returns in new radiance —
Yea, all beauty's deepest melody.

And know: all good that passes away
Is so made that it rises again.

Der Fächer

Das Öffnen eines Fächers sagt, dass sich
Die Welt entfaltet, Schöpfungswunder zeigend:
Oder wie sich die Göttin offenbart,
Amaterasu, aus dem Meere steigend —

So wie in uns der Geist, der sich entfaltet,
Sein Licht in goldnen Bildern neu gestaltet.
Der Fächer schließt sich, wie ein Sang verklingt;
So wie die Sonne spät im Meer versinkt.

So mag der Geist, nach der Entfaltung Scheinen,
Selig zurückkehrn zu dem Großen Einen.

The Fan

The opening of a fan tells how the world
Unfolds to show the marvels of creation;
Or how the goddess manifests herself,
Amaterasu, rising from the sea —

Just as in us the Spirit, self-unfolding,
Shapes its light anew in golden pictures.
The fan closes upon itself, like a song fading away,
Like the sun sinking late into the sea

So may the Spirit, after its unfolding,
Blissfully return to the Great One.

Ein Lied

Es gibt nicht Größe, die nicht Schönheit wirkt
In ihrem Triebe;
Es gibt nicht Schönheit, die nicht Größe birgt;
So ist die Liebe.

Vielleicht macht Liebe dir das Herze wund
In stillem Leide;
Doch Schönheit wohnt in deines Herzens Grund,
In tiefer Freude.

Sei glücklich, Herz, mit edler Weisheit Wein;
Denn Licht macht trunken.
Der Weise ist mit seinem ganzen Sein
In Gott versunken.

Lass, meine Seele, diese Welt verwehn
In Gottes Weiten;
In letzter Liebe will das Herz vergehn —
In Ewigkeiten.

A Song

There is no greatness that begets not beauty
        In its striving;
There is no beauty without greatness;
        Such is love.

Perhaps love wounds thy heart
        In silent pain;
But beauty dwells in thy heart's depth
        In profound joy.

Be happy, heart, with noble wisdom's wine;
        For Light inebriates.
The wise man with his whole being
        Is drowned in God.

Let, O my soul, this world fade away
        In God's infinity;
The heart will melt in ultimate love —
        For all eternity.

Index of First Lines
German and English

A black dot in a white field, and	127
A black holy man once said to me:	45
A sun star — unimaginably great;	125
A winter fairy-tale. Snow covers the land —	75
Ad astra — to the stars — the soul is striving,	5
Ad astra — zu den Sternen — strebt die Seele,	4
Als Lallā Yogīshwarī Ātmā fand	128
An eye that opens and then closes	15
Aus Wahrheit ist das Herz gemacht	72
Because Thou art my God, I call Thee	13
Beim Rätsel "ich" hat oft mein Sinn geweilt.	76
Belovèd human beings are written in the stars,	23
Birth and death — two shores, and a sea	141
Da draußen vor dem Tore,	18
Das Leben, sagt man, geht dem Tod entgegen;	140
Das Öffnen eines Fächers sagt, dass sich	144
Das Weltrad dreht sich, und du bist die Mitte	110
Dasein, dann nicht mehr dasein; Wirklichkeit,	142
Dein Name ist ein wundersamer Laut	132
Dem Reich der Gnosis gleicht der Sternenhimmel —	78
Der Friede Gottes wartet vor der Tür	116
Der Morgen schauert über den Zypressen,	16
Der Morgenstern erhebt sich aus der Nacht	94
Der Schöpfer hat die weite Erdenwelt	8
Der Traube Saft, gekeltert und gegoren,	62
Der Weg zum Höchsten Gut ist eine Brücke;	36
Des Daseins Grund: es gibt ein Urbild Mensch,	108
Des ganzen Veda ungeheurer Strom	130
Des Wahren Strahlung, heißt es, ist im Schönen,	104
Dichten ist Botschaft — oder bloße Kunst,	100
Die Jungfrau: "mit der Sonne nur bekleidet",	98
Die Krähen fliehen —	88
Die Menschen scheinen auf der Flucht zu sein —	112
Die Seel ist ein Geweb von tausend Fragen;	38

Die Unterscheidung zwischen Wirklichkeit und Schein;	26
Die Welt, ein tausendfaches Maskenspiel —	84
Dies musst du lernen: dich am Höchsten Gut	70
Discernment between Reality and appearance;	27
Do not ask thyself what is going to happen.	117
Do you see the birds migrating to the south?	37
Dream-veil world: who can understand thy play?	121
Drei Dinge sind mir heilig: erst die Wahrheit,	26
Du bist mein Gott, und ich rufe Dich —	132
Du wähnst, da sei ein Leben, doch bedenke	66
Du, der du einsam betest, denke nicht	110
Ein Auge, das sich öffnet und sich schließt —	14
Ein schwarzer Punkt in einem weißen Feld,	126
Ein schwarzer Wāli hat mir einst gesagt	44
Ein Sonnenstern — unvorstellbare Größe;	124
Ein Wintermärchen. Schnee bedeckt das Land	74
Erhabenheit ist wie die reine Luft	90
Es floss aus meinem Herzen mancher Sang;	2
Es gibt nicht Größe, die nicht Schönheit wirkt	146
Gebet aus Stein: dies ist das hohe Münster,	46
Geburt und Tod — zwei Ufer und ein Meer	140
Gegrüßt sei mir der tiefe, wilde Wald —	136
Geliebte Menschen stehen in den Sternen	22
Gespräch mit Gott. Er wird dir Antwort geben,	134
Habt ihr gesehen, wie die Seifenblase	112
Have ye seen how the soap bubble,	113
I am neither Moslem, Jew, nor Christian;	43
I dreamt an unknown bard	93
I heard a lute deep in the night —	41
I live now, in this instant,	139
Ich bin nicht Muslim, Jude oder Christ;	42
Ich hörte eine Laute in der Nacht —	40
Ich lebe jetzt, in diesem Augenblick —	138
If thou wilt not journey to the summit for thyself,	35
If we did not suffer in this world,	87
Ihr meint, ich sei der Sänger, weil ich singe —	100
Im Reinen Sein war eine Möglichkeit,	24

In a world where all faith is disappearing,   115
In einer Welt, wo aller Glaube schwindet,   114
In Pure Being there was a possibility   25
In Tibet's art: the golden Divine Pair —   103
In Tibets Kunst: das goldne Götterpaar —   102
Is not the world a mirror in which God   53
Ist nicht die Welt ein Spiegel, in dem Gott   52
Life, it is said, is a movement towards death;   141
Jugendzeit — schon fern, vorbei —   68
Krishna saw his own self — as the Infinite —   61
Lass der Wahrheit lichtes Schwert durchschneiden   82
Let me greet the deep and wild forest   137
Let truth's bright sword cut through   83
Like sparks that spray out of the fire,   21
Man könnt das Paradies als einen Kreis beschreiben: 96
Men always seem to be fleeing —   113
Mermaids bewitch fishermen with songs,   55
Mir träumt, ein fremder Spielmann stand   92
Mit vielen Dingen leben, selbst ein Ding,   30
Morning shivers over the cypresses,   17
My mind has often dwelt on the enigma "I",   77
Mysterium der Geduld: Leid und Verdruss   114
Mystery of patience: the sorrow and vexation   115
Nixen bezaubern Fischer mit Gesang   54
Nur Ein Mensch steht vor Gott und ruft Ihn an,   34
O Nachtigall in süßer Sommernacht —   64
O nightingale, in sweetest summer night —   65
O signs of nature that teach us —   49
O Zeichen der Natur, die uns belehren —   48
Ohn Selbstbeherrschung ist kein Edelmut;   90
On the one hand, you stand alone before God;   107
One could describe Paradise as a circle   97
Only one human being stands before God and invokes Him,   35
Out of my heart flowed many songs;   3
Outside, by the gate,   19
Poetry is a message — or else merely art,   101
Prayer in stone: such is the tall cathedral,   47

Sag einmal: Gott — und tausend eitle Taten 28
Säh ich dich tanzen, Leila, wär mein Herz 58
Say but once: God — and a thousand vain deeds 29
Securitas — man ist vom Wahn besessen 84
Securitas — people are obsessed with the illusion 85
Sein eignes Selbst — als das Unendliche — 60
Serenity is like the pure air 91
She, who brings the stream of thought to silence, 131
Sie denken an Gott und sie zählen 118
Sie, die des Denkens Fluss zum Schweigen bringt, 130
Sieh einerseits: du stehst allein vor Gott; 106
Siehst du die Vögel nach dem Süden ziehn? 36
So wie die Funken aus dem Feuer sprühen, 20
Space and time are infinite — 123
Stand upon the ground 87
Steh du auf deinem Boden 86
Stelle dir nicht die Frag: was wird geschehen? 116
Stille in Gott — ich könnte endlos dich 72
Stillness in God — I could endlessly 73
Talk to God. He will answer thee, 135
Tatsächlich liebt der eine Mensch den andern; 56
The Creator clothed the wide world 9
The crows take flight — 89
The heart is made of Truth 73
The Holy Virgin is primordial and universal woman; 99
The immense river of the whole Veda 131
The juice of the grape, pressed and fermented, 63
The Morning Star arises from the night, 95
The opening of a fan tells how the world 145
The path to the Highest Good is a bridge; 37
The Peace of God is waiting at the door 117
The splendor of the true, it is said, is in the beautiful, 105
The realm of gnosis is like the starry heavens — 79
The ground of existence: there is a human archetype 109
The soul is woven of a thousand questions; 39
The Virgin: "clothed with the sun alone," 99
The world, a thousandfold play of masks — 85

The world-wheel turns, and thou art the center 111
There is no greatness that begets not beauty 147
There is no nobility without self-mastery; 91
There is no time in the nature of God; 13
They think of God and count 119
This must thou learn: wholly to rejoice 71
Thou art my God, and I call Thee — 133
Thou art deceived in thinking that there is one life; 67
Thou who prayest in solitude, think not 111
Three things are sacred to me: firstly Truth; 27
Thy Name is a wondrous sound, 133
Time of youth — already past and gone — 69
To exist, then to exist no more; reality, 143
To live with many things, to be oneself a thing, 31
Traumschleier Welt: wer kann dein Spiel verstehen? 120
Truth and Devotion. Truth is the light 11
Unendlich ist der Raum, die Zeit — 122
Urweib und Allweib ist die Heilge Jungfrau; 98
Wahrheit und Andacht. Wahrheit ist das Licht 10
Warum hat Gott die Sprache uns geschenkt? 32
Was du auch lieben magst, du liebst das Selbst 56
Was ist es, was die Seel nach Innen ruft? 6
Weil Du mein Gott bist, ruf ich Dich — 12
Weltliche Philosophen bauen Thesen — 80
Wenn der Indianer spricht vom Großen Geist 30
Wenn wir in dieser Welt nicht leiden würden, 86
Were I to see thee dance, Leila, my heart 59
What is it that calls the soul inward? 7
Whatever thou mayest love, thou lovest the Self 57
When one human being loves another, 57
When Lallā Yogīshwarī found Ātmā 129
When the Indian speaks of the Great Spirit 51
Why did God give us the gift of speech? 33
Willst du nicht für dich selbst zum Gipfel wandern, 34
Worldly philosophers construct their theses — 81
Ye think I am the singer, because I sing — 101
Zeit kann es nicht im Gotteswesen geben; 12

BY THE SAME AUTHOR

The Transcendent Unity of Religions, *1953*
Revised Edition, *1975, 1984*, *The Theosophical Publishing House, 1993*

Spiritual Perspectives and Human Facts, *1954, 1969*
New Translation, *Perennial Books, 1987*

Gnosis: Divine Wisdom, *1959, 1978, Perennial Books 1990*

Language of the Self, *1959* Revised Edition, *World Wisdom Books, 1999*

Stations of Wisdom, *1961, 1980*
Revised Translation, *World Wisdom Books, 1995*

Understanding Islam, *1963, 1965, 1972, 1976, 1979, 1981, 1986, 1989*
Revised Translation, *World Wisdom Books, 1994, 1998*

Light on the Ancient Worlds, *1966, World Wisdom Books, 1984*

In the Tracks of Buddhism, *1968, 1989*
New Translation, Treasures of Buddhism, *World Wisdom Books, 1993*

Logic and Transcendence, *1975, Perennial Books, 1984*

Esoterism as Principle and as Way, *Perennial Books, 1981, 1990*

Castes and Races, *Perennial Books, 1959, 1982*

Sufism: Veil and Quintessence, *World Wisdom Books, 1981*

From the Divine to the Human, *World Wisdom Books, 1982*

Christianity/Islam, *World Wisdom Books, 1985*

The Essential Writings of Frithjof Schuon (S.H. Nasr, Ed.), *1986,*
Element, 1991

Survey of Metaphysics and Esoterism, *World Wisdom Books, 1986, 2000*

In the Face of the Absolute, *World Wisdom Books, 1989, 1994*

The Feathered Sun: Plains Indians in Art & Philosophy,
World Wisdom Books, 1990

To Have a Center, *World Wisdom Books, 1990*

Roots of the Human Condition, *World Wisdom Books, 1991*

Images of Primordial & Mystic Beauty: Paintings by Frithjof Schuon,
Abodes, 1992

Echoes of Perennial Wisdom, *World Wisdom Books, 1992*

The Play of Masks, *World Wisdom Books, 1992*

Road to the Heart, *World Wisdom Books, 1995*

The Transfiguration of Man, *World Wisdom Books, 1995*

The Eye of the Heart, *World Wisdom Books, 1997*

Form and Substance in the Religions, *World Wisdom, 2002 (in preparation)*